Keto Ice Cream: 40 Tasty Low-Carb Homemade Keto-Friendly Ice Cream Recipes for Health Eating and Weight Loss

Julia Patel

Published by Julia Patel, 2020.

Table of Contents

INTRODUCTION 1
CHAPTER 1: ABOUT KETO-FRIENDLY ICE CREAM 3
   Keto Ice Cream Ingredients 5
   How To Make Keto Ice Cream – Manually Or With Ice Cream Maker 6
   How To Store Keto Ice Cream 7
CHAPTER 2: FRUITY ICE CREAM RECIPES 8
   Blueberry Ice Cream 9
   5-Minute Berry Ice Cream 11
   Strawberry Ice Cream 13
   Yogo-Berry Popsicles 15
   Raspberry Chocolate Chunks Ice Cream 17
   Roasted Strawberry Popsicles 19
   Strawberry Mango Yogurt Popsicles 21
   Raspberry Ice Cream 23
   Strawberry Rhubarb Ice Cream 25
   Lemon Ice Cream 27
   Lime & Berries Popsicles 29
   Berry Popsicles 31
   Lemon Raspberry Popsicles 33
CHAPTER 3: CHOCOLATE AND COFFEE ICE CREAM RECIPES 35
   Dark Chocolate Ice Cream 36
   Coffee Ice Cream 38
   Mint Mocha Ice Cream 40
   No-Churn Chocolate Ice Cream 42
   Chocolate Peanut Butter Ice Cream 44
   Chocolate Avocado Ice Cream 46
   Mocha Ice Cream 48
CHAPTER 4: OTHER ICE CREAM RECIPES 50
   Avocado Lime Coconut Popsicles 51

Avocado Coconut Ice Cream	53
Lime Avocado Sorbet	55
Avocado Pistachio & Matcha Ice Cream	57
Lime & Avocado Popsicles	59
Coconut, Lime & Cilantro Ice Cream	61
Mint Avocado Ice Cream	63
Pumpkin Pecan Ice Cream	65
Sugar Free Mint Ice Cream	67
Vanilla Ice Cream	69
Dairy-Free Vanilla Ice Cream	71
Vanilla Mascarpone Ice Cream	73
Cottage Cheese Peanut Butter Ice Cream	75
Coconut Ice Cream	77
Cookie Dough Ice Cream	79
Cookies And Crème Ice Cream	81
Brown Butter Pecan Ice Cream	83
Butterscotch Sea Salt Ice Cream	85
Mason Jar Ice Cream	87
Turmeric Popsicles	89
MEASUREMENT TABLES	91
CONCLUSION	92

INTRODUCTION

I congratulate you on choosing the cookbook **"Keto Ice Cream"**, which will help you cook low-carb frozen sweets for any holidays and every day.

When you are on a keto diet, you have to part ways with high carb-heavy food. These are the main rules of the game.

Luckily, those following the fat-blasting diet actually don't have to completely say "goodbye" to ice cream.

That is why it is time to make healthy and keto-friendly ice cream at home.

Once you get the hang of making keto ice cream, feel free to experiment with the different ice cream bases, preparation methods, and keto-friendly ingredients to make even more delicious ice cream flavors.

This cookbook contains simple and tasty recipes for making healthy homemade ice cream of the available ingredients.

Each recipe contains a photo of a ready dish and information about important nutrients.

CHAPTER 1: ABOUT KETO-FRIENDLY ICE CREAM

Craving something sweet on a Keto Diet? When you are support this kind of a Diet, the main question is, "Can I eat ice cream?" Actually, the answer is yes, you can.

In this book, we will talk about keto-friendly homemade ice cream recipes that you can easily prepare in your own kitchen.

You get three "Yes" and that is why:
- Yes, You can use Keto-friendly Ingredients for making frozen sweets
- Yes, You can make Ice Cream at any time when you want
- Yes, Keto Ice Cream is super low in carbs per one serving

The next important question: Is it possible to make keto ice cream without an ice cream maker? Yes! You can make homemade low carb ice cream recipe without an ice cream maker if you don't have one.

However, you can also use an ice cream maker if you do have one. I will show you how to make keto ice cream both ways!

KETO ICE CREAM INGREDIENTS

For making homemade keto ice cream, you can to use only keto ingredients for the base:

- Butter
- Ghee
- Coconut Butter (Oil)
- Cocoa Butter
- Heavy cream
- Almond milk
- Coconut milk
- Olive Oil
- Avocado Oil
- Macadamia Oil
- MCT oil
- Yogurt
- Sweeteners (allulose, erythritol, stevia, xylitol)

Besides, you can add favorite keto-friendly toppings in ice cream base. Here are some toppings you add to create your own unique flavors:

- Sugar-free dark chocolate or cacao chips
- Nuts
- Berries
- Coffee
- Cocoa powder
- Vanilla extract
- Mint extract
- Spices
- Lemons and limes

HOW TO MAKE KETO ICE CREAM – MANUALLY OR WITH ICE CREAM MAKER

You can make homemade keto ice cream manually or using an ice cream maker. It all depends on your preferences and technical capabilities.

How to Make Homemade Ice Cream Manually

All you need is ingredients for ice cream, as well as kitchen equipment (mixer, blender or food processor, freezing container, whisk and spoon).

The whole process includes the following steps:

Step 1: Prep Recipe's Ingredients
Step 2: Mix to get Ice cream Base
Step 3: Pre-Freeze
Step 4: Mix and re-freeze

How to Make Homemade Ice Cream with any Types of Ice Cream Maker

You can make any type of homemade keto ice cream easily and faster with an Ice Cream Maker.

Simply transfer the ice cream mass to ice cream maker and let it churn to desired consistency. It typically takes 20-30 minutes; just follow your manufacturer's instructions.

After churning, you can eat the soft-serve ice cream as-is. Otherwise, transfer to freezer container and freeze for a few more hours to get more firm keto friendly ice cream.

HOW TO STORE KETO ICE CREAM

You can store homemade keto ice cream just as you would any other ice cream – in the freezer.

Homemade ice cream stored at -10°C (14°F) has a shelf life of about 1 week, whereas storage at -20°C (-4°F) and -25°C (-13°F) has a shelf life of about 7 to 30 weeks respectively.

Now when you made your keto ice cream, here are several rules for making sure it stays tasty in the freezer:

1. Keep an optimal storage temperature in the freezer
2. Use only airtight storage containers
3. Store ice cream only in the back of the freezer, not in the door
4. Follow the shelf life for homemade ice cream

CHAPTER 2: FRUITY ICE CREAM RECIPES

BLUEBERRY ICE CREAM

Servings: 6
Cooking Time: 15 minutes + 1.5 hours for freezing
Ingredients:

- 1 cup (250 ml) heavy cream
- 3 egg yolks
- 8 oz. (225 g) mascarpone cheese
- 6 oz. (180 g) fresh or frozen blueberries
- 1 tbsp. erythritol powder
- ½ tsp vanilla extract
- ½ tsp ground cardamom
- ½ tsp lemon peel

Cooking process:

1. Prepare the berries. If you use fresh berries, rinse them thoroughly. Frozen berries just get out of the freezer. Whip the

cream until soft and set aside.
2. In a bowl, beat egg yolks, sweetener, vanilla, cardamom and lemon peel until fluffy. Add the mascarpone cheese and the whipped cream.
3. Add the blueberries. Pour the mass into a container with a lid and place in the freezer.
4. Stir the ice cream every fifteen minutes until it firms up. This takes about 1-1.5 hours.

Nutrients per one serving:
Calories: 317 | Fats: 28 g | Carbs: 6 g | Proteins: 5 g

5-MINUTE BERRY ICE CREAM

Servings: 2
Cooking Time: 2 minutes + 3 minutes for cooling
Ingredients:

- 1 cup (250 ml) fresh or frozen fruits to taste
- ½ cup (125 ml) heavy cream
- ½ tsp stevia powder

Cooking process:

1. Add all fruits to a food processor. Mix for 1 minute until smooth.
2. Add the heavy cream and stevia; continue to mix for another 1 minute until the ice cream smooth.
3. Pour into container and cool in the fridge for 3 minutes. Serve it.

Nutrients per one serving:

Calories: 223 | Fats: 20 g | Carbs: 5 g | Proteins: 2 g

STRAWBERRY ICE CREAM

Servings: 6
Cooking Time: 45 minutes + 6 hours for freezing
Ingredients:

- 1 cup (250 ml) heavy cream
- 3 egg yolks
- ⅓ cup (80 ml) erythritol
- ½ tsp vanilla extract
- ¼ tsp xanthan gum
- 1 cup (250 ml) fresh or frozen strawberries

Cooking process:

1. Set a pot with heavy cream onto a low heat to preheat for 2 minutes. Add erythritol.
2. Don't let the cream to a boil; just preheat until erythritol is dissolved.
3. In a large bowl, separate egg yolks from their whites. Beat them

with an electric mixer until smooth.
4. Then, add in a few tablespoons of hot cream mass at a time to the eggs while beating.
5. Do this until the egg mixture is warm and then slowly add in the rest of the cream, beating constantly. Add vanilla extract and mix again.
6. Add xanthan gum, which help the consistency of the ice cream stay creamy.
7. Place bowl into the freezer to chill for about 1-2 hours, stirring occasionally.
8. When the ice cream is chilled and getting a bit thicker, it is time to add the strawberries. Mix strawberries until smooth. Add in the strawberry mass to the chilled cream.
9. Let this strawberry ice cream chill for another 4 hours in the freezer. Then when you are ready to enjoy, let the ice cream temper on the counter for a few minutes and scoop.

Nutrients per one serving:
Calories: 177 | Fats: 16.5 g | Carbs: 2.8 g | Proteins: 2.6 g

YOGO-BERRY POPSICLES

Servings: 6
Cooking Time: 15 minutes + 6 hours for freezing
Ingredients:

- 1 cup (250 ml) fresh or frozen berries to taste
- ⅔ cup (150 ml) sugar-free Greek yogurt
- ⅔ cup (150 ml) coconut cream
- 2 tbsps. granulated stevia
- 6 popsicle molds and sticks

Cooking process:

1. In a bowl, mash the berries and sweetener using a fork.
2. Add the coconut cream and yogurt.
3. Mix to uniformity and pour into popsicle molds. Insert wooden sticks into each of them.
4. Freeze at least for 5-6 hours or overnight.

Nutrients per one serving:
Calories: 87 | Fats: 6.5 g | Carbs: 3.5 g | Proteins: 2.3 g

RASPBERRY CHOCOLATE CHUNKS ICE CREAM

Servings: 5
Cooking Time: 20 minutes + 2 hours for freezing
Ingredients:

- 1 cup (250 ml) heavy cream
- 2 cups (500 ml) fresh or frozen raspberries
- 1 tbsp. chocolate chunks
- ⅓ cup (75 ml) erythritol powder

Cooking process:

1. Pour the cream into a blender. Blend until thick peaks form. In addition, you can use a hand mixer if it is powerful enough.
2. Add the raspberries and sweetener to the blender. Mix until smooth well. Adjust sweetener to taste if needed. Add the chocolate chunks and mix again.

3. This ice cream you can eat as a soft-serve base. If you prefer more dense ice cream, you can run the mass through an ice cream maker, or place in the freezer to firm up. If using the freezer, stir every 30 minutes for the first 2 hours.

Nutrients per one serving:
Calories: 183 | Fats: 16 g | Carbs: 5 g | Proteins: 1 g

ROASTED STRAWBERRY POPSICLES

Servings: 4
Cooking Time: 40 minutes + 4 hours for freezing
Ingredients:

- 2 cups (500 ml) fresh strawberries
- 1 tbsp. olive oil
- 2 tbsps. lemon juice
- 1 cup (250 ml) water
- 4 popsicle molds and sticks

Cooking process:

1. Preheat the oven to 350ºF (175ºC) and cover the baking sheet with parchment paper.
2. Wash the strawberries and cut in half. Toss the fruit in the olive oil and spread it out on the prepared baking sheet. Bake for 45

minutes.
3. Transfer the roasted fruit to a blender and add the remaining ingredients. Mix on high speed until smooth.
4. Pour the base into popsicle molds. Insert wooden sticks in each molds and freeze for 4 hours or overnight.
5. Before serving, place the bottom of the molds in warm water to extract ice cream.

Nutrients per one serving:
Calories: 84 | Fats: 2 g | Carbs: 2.4 g | Proteins: 1 g

STRAWBERRY MANGO YOGURT POPSICLES

Servings: 8
Cooking Time: 10 minutes + 2 hours for freezing
Ingredients:

- 7 oz. (200 g) diced mango
- 7 oz. (200 g) fresh or frozen strawberries
- 1 cup (250 ml) fat Greek yogurt
- ½ cup (125 ml) heavy cream
- 1 tsp vanilla extract
- 8 popsicle molds and sticks

Cooking process:

1. Let mango and strawberries thaw for 10 minutes.
2. Add all the ingredients into a blender and mix until smooth.
3. Pour into popsicle molds, insert wooden sticks in each of them, and let freeze for 2 hours.

Nutrients per one serving:
Calories: 85 | Fats: 5 g | Carbs: 5 g | Proteins: 2 g

RASPBERRY ICE CREAM

Servings: 14
Cooking Time: 35 minutes + 4 hour for freezing
Ingredients:

- 1 cup (250 ml) heavy cream
- 2 cups (500 ml) fresh or frozen raspberries
- 7 oz. (200 g) erythritol
- 3 tbsps. Greek yogurt

Cooking process:

1. Place frozen raspberries in a bowl. Leave to thaw at room temperature about 30 minutes to an hour. If you use fresh berries, just wash up them under cool water.
2. In a separate bowl, mix heavy cream and yogurt. Refrigerate for 30 minutes.
3. Place raspberries into a blender and mix until smooth. Pass

through a fine-meshed strainer to remove all seeds.
4. Add sweetener and mix again until dissolved.
5. Pour raspberry mixture onto the cream mass. Mix until homogeneous. Refrigerate for at least 3 hours.
6. Using an ice cream maker, churn per manufacturer's instructions.

Nutrients per one serving:
Calories: 73 | Fats: 5.4 g | Carbs: 4.04 g | Proteins: 1.2 g

STRAWBERRY RHUBARB ICE CREAM

Servings: 6
Cooking Time: 30 minutes + 3 hours for freezing
Ingredients for sauce:

- ½ cup (125 ml) sliced strawberries
- ½ cup (125 ml) diced rhubarb
- 2 tbsps. granulated stevia
- 1 tsp lemon juice
- 1 tbsp. water
- ½ tsp xanthan gum

Ingredients for ice cream:

- 2 cups (500 ml) heavy cream
- ¾ cup (180 ml) almond milk
- ½ cup (125 ml) granulated stevia
- ½ tbsp. vanilla extract

Cooking process:

1. Prepare the sauce. In a saucepan, combine the sweetener and xanthan gum.
2. Gradually whisk in water and lemon juice until smooth.
3. Add strawberries and rhubarb, stirring frequently on to medium heat.
4. Heat mass until the rhubarb softens (about 5 minutes) and then remove from heat. Let sauce cool to room temperature before adding to the ice cream.
5. Prepare the ice cream. In a large bowl, combine heavy cream, vanilla, and sweetener.
6. Using an electric mixer, whip the mass until stiff peaks form.
7. Gradually add the almond milk, blending between each addition. Beat base until it re-thickens slightly.
8. Transfer base to ice cream machine and freeze per manufacturer's instructions.
9. Once the mixture has reached the creamy texture of ice cream, transfer it to a freezer-safe container. Add the strawberry rhubarb sauce and swirl together with a spoon. Cool in freezer for 3 hours before serving, stirring each 30 minutes.

Nutrients per one serving:
Calories: 284 | Fats: 29.1 g | Carbs: 3.6 g | Proteins: 2.65 g

LEMON ICE CREAM

Servings: 6
Cooking Time: 15 minutes + 2 hours for freezing
Ingredients:

- 3 eggs
- 1 lemon
- ⅓ cup (80 ml) erythritol
- 1 ¾ cups (430 ml) heavy cream

Cooking process:

1. Wash the lemon in warm water. Finely grate the peel. Squeeze out the juice and set aside.
2. Separate eggs. Beat egg whites until thick peaks. In another bowl, whisk egg yolks and erythritol until fluffy. Carefully add egg whites and lemon juice into yolk mass.
3. Whip cream in a large bowl until soft peaks form. Add egg mass into cream.

4. Pour into ice cream maker and freeze according to instructions.
5. If you have not an ice cream maker, you can place the bowl in the freezer and give it a good stir every half hour until it reaches the desired consistency. It can take up to 2 hours. If ice cream frozen well, let stand at room temperature for 10 minutes before serving.

Nutrients per one serving:
Calories: 255 | Fats: 23 g | Carbs: 3 g | Proteins: 5 g

LIME & BERRIES POPSICLES

Servings: 6
Cooking Time: 15 minutes + 5 hours for freezing
Ingredients:

- 4 oz. (110 g) fresh or frozen raspberries
- 2 oz. (55 g) fresh or frozen blueberries
- 2 oz. (55 g) fresh or frozen strawberries
- 15 oz. (425 g) whisked coconut milk
- ½ cup (125 ml) water
- 2 tbsps. lime juice
- 1 tsp liquid stevia
- 6 popsicle molds and sticks

Cooking process:

1. Set aside a third of the berries. Add the rest to a bowl and beat until smooth.
2. Pour in coconut milk, water and lime juice. Add a liquid stevia

to taste. Combine all ingredients.
3. Distribute the rest of the berries in the popsicle molds.
4. Pour the ice cream mass into a beaker, then distribute evenly in the molds. Tap the molds on the counter a few times to get rid of air bubbles. Insert the popsicle sticks, and freeze for at least 5 hours.

Tip

If you have any popsicle mass left after pouring into the molds, feel free to freeze it in a separate mold.

Nutrients per one serving:

Calories: 145 | Fats: 15 g | Carbs: 4 g | Proteins: 2 g

BERRY POPSICLES

Servings: 6
Cooking Time: 20 minutes + 4 hours for freezing
Ingredients:

- 1 cup (250 ml) fresh or frozen raspberries
- 1 cup (250 ml) fresh or frozen blueberries
- 1 ½ cups (375 ml) coconut cream
- 1 cup (250 ml) water
- 3 tsp liquid stevia
- ½ tsp vanilla extract
- 6 popsicle molds and sticks for ice cream

Cooking process:

1. In a saucepan, place the raspberries, ½-cup water, and 1-teaspoon liquid stevia. Bring the mass to a boil over medium-high heat. Simmer for about 5 minutes. Remove from the heat and use the blender to make puree.

2. Repeat the above process with the blueberries. In a saucepan, place the blueberries, ½-cup water and 1-teaspoon liquid stevia over medium-high heat. Simmer for about 5 minutes. Remove from the heat and make a puree. Set aside to cool.
3. In a bowl, mix the coconut cream, 1-teaspoon liquid stevia and vanilla extract. Set aside.
4. To assemble the popsicles start by dividing the raspberry puree into the molds. Carefully add approximately 2-3 full tablespoons of base into the center of each mold, filling about ⅓ full. Place the molds into the freezer and chill for at least 1 hour until set.
5. Using the same method divide the coconut cream into the molds, about 3-4 tablespoons in each. Try to work quickly so the raspberry layer does not melt.
6. Place back in the freezer for about 30 minutes. The coconut layer should be firm enough to hold the popsicle sticks but soft enough they can still be inserted.
7. Add one stick to each mold, leaving a little bit of stick poking above the top (to hold it by) and place back into the freezer for at least another hour until completely solid.
8. Finally add the blueberry puree using the same method, about 2-3 full tablespoons in each.
9. Place the molds back in the freezer until completely set, at least another 1 hour.

Nutrients per one serving:
Calories: 146 | Fats: 13.1 g | Carbs: 5.2 g | Proteins: 1.15 g

LEMON RASPBERRY POPSICLES

Servings: 6

Cooking Time: 20 minutes + 2 hours for freezing

Ingredients:

- ½ cup (125 ml) fresh or frozen raspberries
- 1 cup (250 ml) coconut milk
- ¼ cup (60 ml) heavy cream
- ¼ cup (60 ml) sour cream
- ¼ cup (60 ml) coconut oil
- ½ tsp xanthan gum
- 2 tbsps. lemon juice
- 1 tsp liquid stevia
- 6 popsicle molds and sticks for ice cream

Cooking process:

1. Add all ingredients into a container and use the blender to blend together.

2. Continue blending until the berries are completely mixed in with the rest of the ingredients.
3. Strain the mixture, to remove all seeds. Pour the base into popsicle molds and place sticks for ice cream. Set the popsicles in the freezer for a minimum of 2 hours.

Nutrients per one serving:
Calories: 152 | Fats: 16 g | Carbs: 2 g | Proteins: 0.6 g

CHAPTER 3: CHOCOLATE AND COFFEE ICE CREAM RECIPES

DARK CHOCOLATE ICE CREAM

Servings: 4

Cooking Time: 30 minutes + 2 hours for freezing
Ingredients:

- 10 oz. (280 g) sugar free dark chocolate
- 2 ½ cups (375 ml) water
- 6 egg yolks
- 2 tsp vanilla extract
- 2 tbsps. liquid stevia

Cooking process:

1. In the microwave, melt the chocolate with 1 cup water. Stir to uniformity.
2. Mix the egg yolks together. While stirring, add a small part of the hot chocolate mass to the yolks. Add a second part and mix well.

3. Place the chocolate mixture in a blender. Add the vanilla. Mix on low speed and either add the 1 ½ cups ice water bit by bit, blending for a few seconds in between each addition.
4. Place the chocolate mass in an ice cream maker. Churn, following the manufacturer's instructions. Transfer the ice cream into a freezer-safe container and freeze for about 2 hours to get perfect consistency.

Nutrients per one serving:
Calories: 185 | Fats: 5 g | Carbs: 2.6 g | Proteins: 2 g

COFFEE ICE CREAM

Servings: 2

Cooking Time: 25 minutes + 1 hour for cooling
Ingredients:

- 2 ripe peeled and diced avocados
- 1 ½ cup (375 ml) frozen coconut cream
- 2 tbsps. coffee espresso
- 4 tbsps. granulated stevia
- 1 tsp vanilla extract
- 1 tbsp. avocado oil

Cooking process:

1. Remove the frozen coconut cream from the freezer and allow them to thaw slightly for 10 minutes.
2. Add all of your ingredients to a blender or food processor and blend until smooth and creamy. Add avocado oil very slowly

until it forms a smooth ice cream consistency.
3. Taste the ice cream and adjust the sweetness if needed. When it is ready, transfer into bowls and cool for 1 hour.

Nutrients per one serving:
Calories: 485 | Fats: 56 g | Carbs: 4.8 g | Proteins: 6.5 g

MINT MOCHA ICE CREAM

Servings: 6

Cooking Time: 15 minutes + 1.5 hours for freezing

Ingredients:

- 2 cups (500 ml) heavy cream
- 6 egg yolks
- ⅔ cup (160 ml) erythritol powder
- 2 tbsps. chopped sugar-free dark chocolate
- 2 tbsps. coffee powder
- 2 tbsps. vanilla extract
- ½ tsp mint extract
- ½ tsp liquid stevia
- A pinch of salt

Cooking process:

1. In a saucepan over low heat, preheat the heavy cream, stirring with a whisk.

2. Add the chocolate and continue stirring until the chocolate has melted. Add the egg yolks. Continue whisking on low heat until mass warmed.
3. Add an erythritol, coffee powder and whisk until completely dissolved. Continue heating, whisking constantly, until the custard thickens, about 10 minutes.
4. When the custard coats the back of a wooden spoon, remove the pan from the heat. Do not allow the mass to warm to over 145°F (62°C) or the eggs will begin to cook.
5. Stir in the vanilla extract, salt, mint and stevia. Mix well and place in the fridge to cool.
6. When cool, churn the ice cream mixture in an ice cream maker following the manufacturer's directions until it reaches your desired consistency.

Nutrients per one serving:
Calories: 320 | Fats: 25 g | Carbs: 4.2 g | Proteins: 6 g

NO-CHURN CHOCOLATE ICE CREAM

Servings: 10
Cooking Time: 25 minutes + 2 hours for freezing
Ingredients:

- 2 13-oz (368 g) cans canned coconut milk
- 2 ½ oz. (55 g) sugar-free dark chocolate
- 2 tbsps. powder stevia
- 2 tbsps. cocoa powder

Cooking process:

1. Place a small loaf pan in the freezer to chill.
2. In a blender, add chilled coconut milk. Mix for 30 seconds before adding other ingredients. Mix again until creamy mass.
3. Pour the ice cream mass into the frozen loaf pan and spread evenly. Mix ice cream every 30 minutes, for the first 1-2 hours.

4. Once ready to enjoy, allow to thaw at room temperature for 15 minutes. Using a slightly wet ice cream scoop, scoop desired amount into a bowl.

Tips

If ice cream is too frozen, thaw until creamier. If it is still stiff, re-blend for 30 seconds.

Nutrients per one serving:

Calories: 131 | Fats: 11 g | Carbs: 2 g | Proteins: 7 g

CHOCOLATE PEANUT BUTTER ICE CREAM

Servings: 6

Cooking Time: 15 minutes + 3 hours for freezing

Ingredients:

- 1 13-oz (368 g) can fat coconut milk
- ½ cup (125 ml) melted coconut oil
- 4 tbsps. cocoa powder
- 4 tbsps. powder stevia

Cooking process:

1. Place all ingredients in a blender or food processor, mix until smooth.
2. Pour the mass into a 1 ½ or 2 quart (2 liter) glass freezer container.

3. Cover and freeze for 30 minutes, then stir well, especially stirring away from the sides into the center.
4. Cover and freeze for another 30 minutes and stir again. Cover and freeze for 2 hours.
5. Simply thaw on the table for about an hour to soften before eating.

Nutrients per one serving:
Calories: 352 | Fats: 28 g | Carbs: 5 g | Proteins: 6 g

CHOCOLATE AVOCADO ICE CREAM

Servings: 6
Cooking Time: 15 minutes + 8 hours for freezing
Ingredients:

- 2 large avocados
- 1 cup (250 ml) coconut milk
- ½ cup (125 ml) heavy cream
- ½ cup (125 ml) cocoa powder
- ½ cup (125 ml) erythritol powder
- 2 oz. (55 g) sugar-free baker's chocolate
- 2 tsp vanilla extract
- 1 tsp liquid stevia

Cooking process:

1. Cut avocados in half, then scoop out the flesh out into a bowl.

2. Add coconut milk, heavy cream, and vanilla. Use a blender to mix this mass until smooth.
3. Add erythritol, stevia, and cocoa powder to the creamy mass and mix again.
4. Once the mass is smooth, chop baker's chocolate and add into the bowl. Mix again.
5. Leave the bowl in the fridge for 8 hours to completely cool.

Nutrients per one serving:
Calories: 215 | Fats: 19.4 g | Carbs: 3.7 g | Proteins: 3.8 g

MOCHA ICE CREAM

Servings: 2
Cooking Time: 25 minutes
Ingredients:

- 1 cup (250 ml) coconut milk
- ¼ cup (60 ml) heavy cream
- 2 tbsps. cocoa powder
- 1 tbsp. instant coffee
- 2 tbsps. erythritol
- 1 tsp liquid stevia
- ¼ tsp xanthan gum

Cooking process:

1. Add all ingredients except for xanthan gum into a large container.
2. Using an immersion blender, mix all ingredients until smooth. Slowly add in xanthan gum until a slightly thicker mass is

formed.
3. Add ice cream mass to your ice cream machine and follow manufacturer's instructions.
4. When serving, you can add some extra instant coffee to ready ice cream.

Nutrients per one serving:
Calories: 176 | Fats: 14.5 g | Carbs: 6.6 g | Proteins: 2.5 g

CHAPTER 4: OTHER ICE CREAM RECIPES

AVOCADO LIME COCONUT POPSICLES

Servings: 6
Cooking Time: 10 minutes + 4 hours for freezing
Ingredients:

- 2 ripe pitted avocados
- 1 ½ cups (375 ml) coconut milk
- ¼ cup (60 ml) erythritol
- 2 tbsps. lime juice
- 6 popsicle molds and sticks

Cooking process:

1. Place all ingredients into a blender; mix for 2 minute until uniformity.
2. Evenly distribute the base into six popsicle molds with a spoon.
3. Tap the filled molds on the counter top to remove air bubbles and settle the mass.

4. Place popsicle sticks into each of the molds.
5. Freeze the molds for 3-4 hours or until the ice cream has completely solidified.

Nutrients per one serving:
Calories: 218 | Fats: 21 g | Carbs: 7.1 g | Proteins: 2 g

AVOCADO COCONUT ICE CREAM

Servings: 8
Cooking Time: 30 minutes + 3 hour for freezing
Ingredients:

- 1 large avocado
- 1 lime
- 1 cup (250 ml) coconut milk
- ½ cup (125 ml) heavy cream
- ¾ cup (180 ml) erythritol
- 1 cup (250 ml) coconut flakes

Cooking process:

1. Cut avocado lengthwise and remove the pit. Put the flesh of an avocado into a blender.
2. Add coconut milk, heavy cream, and sweetener into a blender. Mix until smooth.

3. Peel lime and squeeze juice. Add lime juice and zest to blender. Mix again for 1 minute. Refrigerate base for at least 1 hour.
4. Preheat pan. Place coconut flakes into the pan. Preheat until lightly brown. Remove pan from heat. Set aside.
5. Transfer avocado ice cream base to the ice cream machine and churn according to manufacturer's directions. Freeze ice cream for 2 hours.
6. When serving, sprinkle with toasted coconut flakes to taste.

Nutrients per one serving:
Calories: 222 | Fats: 21.1 g | Carbs: 6.8 g | Proteins: 2.05 g

LIME AVOCADO SORBET

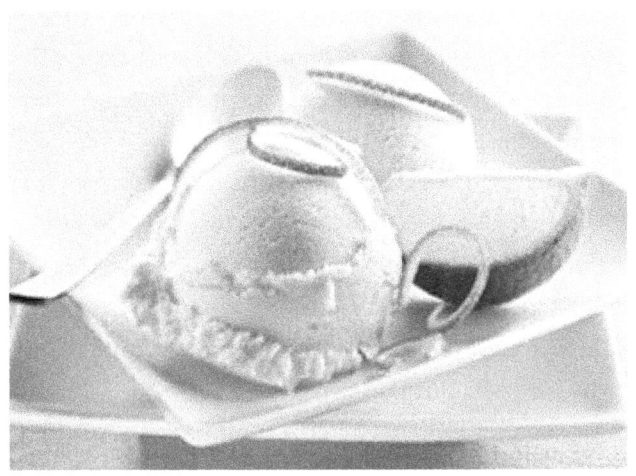

Servings: 4
Cooking Time: 25 minutes + 3 hours for freezing
Ingredients:

- 2 avocados
- 2 limes
- ½ cup (125 ml) chopped cilantro
- 1 cup (250 ml) coconut milk
- ¼ cup (60 ml) erythritol
- ¼ tsp liquid stevia

Cooking process:

1. Slice avocados in half. Remove seeds and cut the flesh into slices. Rest pieces on foil and squeeze juice of half lime.
2. Store avocado in freezer for at least 2 hours. Only start the next step 2 hours after you put the avocado in the freezer.

3. In a pan, bring coconut milk to a boil. Zest all limes while coconut milk is heating up.
4. Once coconut milk is boiling, add lime zest and continue to let the milk reduce in volume.
5. Once you see that the coconut milk is starting to thicken, remove and place into a container. It should have reduced by about 20%.
6. Store the coconut milk mass in the freezer and let it completely cool.
7. Remove avocados from freezer. The lime juice should have helped them not turn brown.
8. Add avocado, cilantro, and juice from 1 ½ lime into the food processor. Mix until uniformity
9. Pour coconut milk mass in the food processor. Add stevia and mix again for 2 minutes.
10. Freeze ice cream for 1 hour and serve it.

Nutrients per one serving:
Calories: 131 | Fats: 11.6 g | Carbs: 3.35 g | Proteins: 1.5 g

AVOCADO PISTACHIO & MATCHA ICE CREAM

Servings: 8

Cooking Time: 30 minutes + 2 hours for freezing
Ingredients:

- ½ cup (125 ml) coconut oil
- ½ cup (125 ml) avocado oil
- 2 cups (500 ml) fat coconut milk
- 4 egg yolks
- 2 ripe peeled and chopped avocados
- ½ cup (125 ml) chopped pistachios
- 2 tbsps. apple vinegar
- 2 tbsps. grass-fed gelatin
- 1 tbsp. matcha powder
- 1 tsp vanilla extract
- ½ tsp cinnamon
- A pinch of sea salt

Cooking process:

1. In a tall container, add the coconut oil, avocado oil, apple vinegar and egg yolks. Insert immersion blender and push it all the way down until it makes contact with the bottom of the bowl, then push the power button and do not move the blender for a full 20 seconds. As the oil starts to emulsify, start moving your blender around and up and down just to make sure that every last bit of oil gets well incorporated. Set it aside.
2. Add the coconut milk, gelatin, matcha powder, vanilla, cinnamon and salt to a large container. Blend well with an immersion blender, until completely smooth.
3. Add the reserved oil base and the flesh of the avocados then blend again until smooth and perfectly combined.
4. Transfer this mass to ice cream maker and churn according to the manufacturer's instructions. When the ice cream is almost set, throw in the chopped pistachios and continue churning until the nuts are evenly distributed.
5. You can serve this ice cream immediately as a soft serve or transfer it to an airtight container and place it in the freezer for 2 hours to firm up.

Nutrients per one serving:
Calories: 258 | Fats: 18.3 g | Carbs: 5.1 g | Proteins: 16 g

LIME & AVOCADO POPSICLES

Servings: 6
Cooking Time: 15 minutes + 3 hours for freezing
Ingredients:

- 2 ripe avocados
- 2 limes
- 1 ½ cups (375 ml) coconut milk
- ½ cup (125 ml) erythritol powder
- 1 tsp liquid stevia
- 6 popsicle molds and sticks

Cooking process:

1. Halve the avocados and remove the bones. Scoop the soft pulp into a bowl.
2. Grate the zest from one lime, and then squeeze the juice from the remaining fruit
3. Add the coconut milk, fresh lime zest and juice, erythritol and

stevia.
4. Using a hand blender, mix all ingredients until smooth. Using a spoon, fill in the popsicle molds and insert wooden sticks into each of them.
5. Place ice cream in the freezer for at least 3 hours or until frozen. Store in the freezer for up to 2 months.

Nutrients per one serving:
Calories: 265 | Fats: 25.3 g | Carbs: 5.2 g | Proteins: 2.9 g

COCONUT, LIME & CILANTRO ICE CREAM

Servings: 12

Cooking Time: 40 minutes + 1 hour for cooling

Ingredients:

- 3 cups (750 ml) fat coconut milk
- 2 tbsps. chopped cilantro
- 2 limes
- 2 ½ tbsps. erythritol

Cooking process:

1. In a bowl, combine the coconut milk and cilantro until smooth. Pour the base into a jar. Cover and leave to infuse for 30 minutes.
2. Strain the mass through a fine mesh sieve, and remove the cilantro.

3. Squeeze the juice from the limes. Stir in the lime juice and erythritol, mix well. Pour the creamy base into the ice-cream maker.
4. Churn the ice cream according to the manufacturer's instructions, transfer into large container, and cool for 1 hour in the fridge.

Nutrients per one serving:
Calories: 89 | Fats: 10 g | Carbs: 1 g | Proteins: 1 g

MINT AVOCADO ICE CREAM

Servings: 4
Cooking Time: 55 minutes + 2 hours for freezing
Ingredients:

- 3 cups (750 ml) fat coconut milk
- 2 cups (500 ml) shopped mint
- 2 ripe avocados
- 1 tsp liquid stevia

Cooking process:

1. Preheat the coconut milk, mint, and stevia in a saucepan over low heat, stirring until hot and steamy. Turn off the heat, cover and let steep for 45 minutes.
2. Halve the avocados, remove the pits, scrape out the flesh and place in a food processor or blender. Pour the coconut milk mass through a mesh strainer into the food processor or

blender. Blend until completely smooth, then refrigerate for at least 2 hours.
3. In addition, you can use ice cream maker for this recipe. Churn and freeze the mass in an ice cream maker according to the manufacturer's directions. Serve immediately or store in the freezer in a plastic or metal container.

Nutrients per one serving:
Calories: 354 | Fats: 25 g | Carbs: 3.8 g | Proteins: 5.9 g

PUMPKIN PECAN ICE CREAM

Servings: 4
Cooking Time: 35 minutes + 30 minutes for cooling
Ingredients:

- ½ cup (125 ml) cottage cheese
- ½ cup (125 ml) pumpkin puree
- 2 cups (500 ml) coconut milk
- 3 egg yolks
- 6 tbsps. chopped toasted pecans
- 2 tbsps. salted butter
- 1 tsp pumpkin spice
- ⅓ cup (80 ml) erythritol
- ½ tsp xanthan gum
- 1 tbsp. liquid stevia

Cooking process:

1. Preheat toasted pecans with butter on the stove over low heat for 2 minutes.
2. Place the rest of the ingredients into a bowl. Using immersion blender, mix them into a smooth mass.
3. Add mass to ice cream machine, as per instructions of manufacturer.
4. Once your butter is browned and the pecans have soaked up some of the butter, place inside of the ice cream machine and continue to cook.
5. Place ready ice cream in the ice cream bowls and cool for 30 minutes.

Nutrients per one serving:
Calories: 286 | Fats: 23.4 g | Carbs: 7.8 g | Proteins: 7.5 g

SUGAR FREE MINT ICE CREAM

Servings: 4
Cooking Time: 25 minutes + 1 hour for freezing
Ingredients:

- 2 cups (500 ml) heavy cream
- ¼ cup (60 ml) almond milk
- 4 egg yolks
- 3 tbsps. peppermint syrup
- 1 tsp stevia powder
- 6 drops green food coloring

Cooking process:

1. In a saucepan, combine cream and almond milk and preheat on the stove above a slow heat for 2 minutes.
2. In another bowl, combine all other ingredients. Add to heated cream and stir well. Preheat slowly until thickened and do not forget for stirring.

3. Strain into a chilled bowl and distribute over volume. Chill in the fridge for 1 hour.
4. Add to ice cream maker, following manufacturer's instructions. Transfer an ice cream to container and store in the freezer.

Nutrients per one serving:
Calories: 223 | Fats: 17 g | Carbs: 4.1 g | Proteins: 6 g

VANILLA ICE CREAM

Servings: 2
Cooking Time: 25 minutes + 2 hours for freezing
Ingredients:

- 1 ½ cups (375 ml) heavy cream
- 2 egg yolks
- 2 egg whites
- 2 tbsps. xylitol
- 1 tsp vanilla powder

Cooking process:

1. In a bowl, whisk the egg yolks until smooth.
2. In a saucepan, combine the cream with the vanilla and the xylitol. Bring to a boil and simmer for 2 minutes, until the cream thickens slightly.
3. Reduce the heat and pour the whipped egg yolks into the

cream. Combine well and simmer on low heat while stirring constantly, until the mass thickens. Cool mass in the fridge for 30 minutes.
4. In a bowl, beat the egg whites until thickness; add them into the cream mass.
5. Pour the batter into an ice cream maker and place in the freezer. Stir occasionally and continue freezing until it reaches desired consistency.

Nutrients per one serving:
Calories: 275 | Fats: 14 g | Carbs: 3.5 g | Proteins: 5.5 g

DAIRY-FREE VANILLA ICE CREAM

Servings: 6
Cooking Time: 10 minutes + 1.1 hours for freezing
Ingredients:

- 1 cup (250 ml) coconut milk
- 1 ¼ cups (310 ml) almond milk
- 6 egg yolks
- ⅓ cup (80 ml) xylitol
- ⅓ cup (80 ml) avocado oil
- 2 tsp vanilla extract
- A pinch of salt

Cooking process:

1. In a saucepan, over low heat, preheat the coconut milk and almond milk, stirring with a whisk. Add the egg yolks. Continue heating on low heat until mass increase.

2. Add the xylitol and whisk until dissolved. Continue heating, whisking constantly, until the custard thickens, about 8-10 minutes.
3. When the custard reaches 145°F (62°C) on a thermometer, remove the pan from the heat. Do not allow the mass to warm to over 145°F (62°C) or the eggs will begin to cook.
4. Add the avocado oil, vanilla, salt, and mix in a blender. Allow the ice cream to cool in the fridge.
5. When the ice cream mass is cool, freeze in an ice cream maker, following the directions. Continue processing the ice cream until it is frozen or reaches your desired consistency. Store in the freezer.

Nutrients per one serving:
Calories: 258 | Fats: 20 g | Carbs: 3 g | Proteins: 7.2 g

VANILLA MASCARPONE ICE CREAM

Servings: 4
Cooking Time: 20 minutes + 2 hours for freezing
Ingredients:

- 5 oz. (140 g) mascarpone cheese
- 5 oz. (140 g) unsalted butter
- 4 eggs
- ½ tsp vanilla extract
- 1 tsp liquid stevia
- ¼ tsp tartar cream

Cooking process:

1. Separate eggs. Preheat egg yolks, cheese, and butter on low heat

whisking frequently until thickened. Remove from heat and stir in sweetener and vanilla.
2. Add tartar cream to egg whites and whip until stiff. Add yolks mixture into egg whites.
3. Pour into freezer container with lid. Place in freezer for 1 hour, then stir frozen base. Place back in freezer for another hour.

Nutrients per one serving:
Calories: 325 | Fats: 31 g | Carbs: 1.5 g | Proteins: 9.6 g

COTTAGE CHEESE PEANUT BUTTER ICE CREAM

Servings: 2
Cooking Time: 10 minutes + 1 hour for freezing
Ingredients:

- 1 cup (250 ml) cottage cheese
- 2 tbsps. heavy cream
- 2 tbsps. peanut butter
- 1 tbsp. chopped nuts (to taste)
- ½ tsp stevia

Cooking process:

1. Put the cottage cheese, stevia and heavy cream into a food processor.
2. Add that peanut butter; mix it up with for one minutes until uniformity. This should aerate the ice cream a little bit, and turn it a lighter color.

3. Separate into two servings. Sprinkle with chopped nuts. Put it into the freezer for 1 hour to cool.

Nutrients per one serving:
Calories: 309 | Fats: 19.4 g | Carbs: 7.9 g | Proteins: 28.7 g

COCONUT ICE CREAM

Servings: 2
Cooking Time: 10 minutes + 1 hour for freezing
Ingredients:

- 2 cups (500 ml) coconut milk
- ⅓ cup (80 ml) stevia
- 1 ½ tsp vanilla extract
- ⅛ tsp salt

Cooking process:

1. In a bowl, mix coconut milk, sweetener, salt and vanilla extract.
2. If you have an ice cream maker, just churn according to the manufacturer's instructions.
3. If you want to make it without an ice cream machine, freeze the mixture in the containers for 1 hour, then mix the frozen mass in a blender until uniformity. Then freeze for another 1 hour before serving.

Nutrients per one serving:
Calories: 136 | Fats: 10.1 g | Carbs: 4.8 g | Proteins: 19.8 g

COOKIE DOUGH ICE CREAM

Servings: 4
Cooking Time: 35 minutes + 2 hours for freezing
Ingredients for cookie dough:

- ⅓ cup (80 ml) almond flour
- 2 tbsps. softened butter
- 2 tbsps. xylitol
- 1 tbsp. sugar-free chopped chocolate
- ½ tsp vanilla extract

Ingredients for ice cream:

- 1 ½ cups (375 ml) heavy cream
- 1 cup (250 ml) almond milk
- 5 eggs yolks
- ½ cup (125 ml) xylitol
- 2 tsp vanilla powder

- ½ tsp salt

Cooking process:

1. Prepare the ice cream. In a saucepan, preheat the cream and almond milk on low heat, slowly stirring with a whisk. Add the egg yolks and beat until frothy.
2. Continue whisking on low heat until the mass reaches a temperature of 145°F (62°C) or until the mass thickens.
3. Add the xylitol to the cream mass and whisk until well dissolved. Add the vanilla and salt. Remove from heat and cool it in the fridge. While the ice cream mass cools, make the cookie dough.
4. Prepare the cookie dough. Combine all ingredients and mix them well.
5. Crumble the dough into small pieces. Set aside.
6. Take the ice cream mass from the fridge and add it to ice cream maker. Follow the manufacturer's directions for making ice cream.
7. While the ice cream is still churning and soft, gradually add the cookie dough bits to the ice cream mass. As the ice cream churns, the cookie dough bits will be distributed through the mass.
8. Let the ice cream continue to making in the ice cream maker until it is ready to be served, or stored in the freezer.

Tips

To give the ice cream a creamier consistency once frozen, use xylitol instead of erythritol or an erythritol blend. Erythritol makes the ice cream very hard; however, if you use erythritol, simply wait 5 minutes to serve the ice cream after removing it from the freezer.

Nutrients per one serving:
Calories: 128 | Fats: 12.5 g | Carbs: 1.8 g | Proteins: 2.7 g

COOKIES AND CRÈME ICE CREAM

Servings: 10
Cooking Time: 40 minutes + 2 hours for freezing
Ingredients for cookies:

- ¾ cup (180 ml) almond flour
- 1 egg
- ¼ cup (60 ml) cocoa powder
- ¼ cup (60 ml) erythritol
- ¼ tsp baking powder
- ½ tsp vanilla extract
- 1 ½ tbsps. softened coconut oil

Ingredients for ice cream:

- 2 ½ cups (625 ml) heavy cream
- ½ cup (125 ml) almond milk
- ½ cup (125 ml) erythritol

- 1 tbsp. vanilla extract

Cooking process:

1. Preheat oven to 300°F (150°C). Line 8-inch circular cake pan with parchment paper and spray with oil.
2. Sift the almond flour, cocoa powder, baking powder, erythritol into a bowl and whisk until smooth.
3. Add the vanilla extract and coconut oil and mix until batter forms into fine crumbs.
4. Add the egg and blend until cookie batter begins to stick together and form a ball.
5. Transfer the batter into prepared cake pan and press out batter carefully with your fingers until it evenly covers the bottom of the pan. Place cake pan in preheated oven and bake for 20 minutes.
6. When finished baking, remove cake pan from oven and let cool. Once the cookie has cooled, break the cookie into small crumbles.
7. In a bowl, blend the heavy cream with a mixer until stiff peaks form. Add vanilla extract and erythritol, and whip until smooth. Pour in almond milk and blend mass until it re-thickens.
8. Transfer cream mass to ice cream maker and churn until ice cream begins to hold its shape. Gradually add the cookie crumbles into ice cream mass.
9. Once all of the cookie crumbles are incorporated, then transfer the ice cream into a freezer-safe container and freeze for at least 2 hours before serving.

Nutrients per one serving:
Calories: 280 | Fats: 28.6 g | Carbs: 3 g | Proteins: 4.6 g

BROWN BUTTER PECAN ICE CREAM

Servings: 3

Cooking Time: 30 minutes + 1 hour for cooling

Ingredients:

- 1 ½ cups (375 ml) coconut milk
- ¼ cup (60 ml) heavy cream
- ¼ cup (60 ml) chopped pecans
- 5 tbsps. butter
- 1 tsp liquid stevia
- ¼ tsp xanthan gum

Cooking process:

1. In a pan over low heat, stir butter until melted and begins to turn a deep amber color.

2. Once butter is browned, add heavy cream, pecans, and stevia. Stir well.
3. Add coconut milk, butter mass, and xanthan gum to a container. Mix well with a whisk until uniformity.
4. Add ice cream mass to your ice cream machine and cook according to manufacturer's instructions.

Nutrients per one serving:
Calories: 355 | Fats: 36.3 g | Carbs: 4.4 g | Proteins: 2.1 g

BUTTERSCOTCH SEA SALT ICE CREAM

Servings: 3
Cooking Time: 25 minutes + 1 hour for cooling
Ingredients:

- 1 cup (250 ml) coconut milk
- ¼ cup (60 ml) heavy cream
- ¼ cup (60 ml) sour cream
- 3 tbsps. butter
- 2 tsp butterscotch flavoring
- 2 tbsps. erythritol
- 1 tsp liquid stevia
- ½ tsp xanthan gum
- ½ tsp flaked sea salt

Cooking process:

1. In a container, mix coconut milk, sour cream, heavy cream, butterscotch flavoring, sweeteners, salt, and guar gum. Use an immersion blender to blend ingredients until uniformity.
2. In a pan over low heat, preheat the butter until an amber color.
3. Add butter to your ice cream base and use your immersion blender again to blend ingredients together.
4. Add ice cream mass to ice cream machine and let churn according to manufacturer's instructions.

Nutrients per one serving:
Calories: 274 | Fats: 24.7 g | Carbs: 4.1 g | Proteins: 1.5 g

MASON JAR ICE CREAM

Servings: 1
Cooking Time: 5 minutes + 2 hours for freezing
Ingredients:

- ½ cup (125 ml)
- 1 egg yolk
- 1 tbsp. xylitol
- ½ tsp vanilla powder
- Mason jar

Cooking process:

1. For making Mason Jar Ice Cream, you need to use a Mason jar or similar glass jar with a lid. Combine all ingredients in the jar, seal the lid and shake for 3-5 minutes.

2. Place the jar into the freezer for 2 hours.

Nutrients per one serving:
Calories: 232 | Fats: 22 g | Carbs: 5 g | Proteins: 6 g

TURMERIC POPSICLES

Servings: 4
Cooking Time: 10 minutes + 5 hours for freezing
Ingredients:

- 1 cup (250 ml) coconut milk
- ½ tbsp. turmeric powder
- 1 tsp ginger powder
- 1 tbsp. liquid stevia
- 4 popsicle molds and sticks

Cooking process:

1. In a small saucepan, preheat up the coconut milk; melt the sweetener and spices into it.
2. Combine well and pour into popsicle molds. Insert wooden sticks in each of them.
3. Place the ice cream into the freezer and freeze for 5 hours.

Nutrients per one serving:
Calories: 108 | Fats: 11 g | Carbs: 2 g | Proteins: 1.2 g

MEASUREMENT TABLES

US Customary Quantity	Metric
1 teaspoon	5 ml
1 tablespoon	15 ml
2 tablespoons	30 ml
1/4 cup *or* 2 fluid ounces	60 ml
1/3 cup	80 ml
1/2 cup *or* 4 fluid ounces	125 ml
2/3 cup	160 ml
3/4 cup *or* 6 fluid ounces	180 ml
1 cup *or* 8 fluid ounces *or* 1/2 pint	250 ml
1 1/2 cup *or* 12 fluid ounces	375 ml
2 cups *or* 1 pint *or* 16 fluid ounces	500 ml
3 cups *or* 1 1/2 pints	700 mL
4 cups *or* 2 pints *or* 1 quart	950 ml

°C (CELSIUS)	F° (FAHRENHEIT)
140	275
150	300
165	325
175	350
190	375
200	400
220	425
230	450
240	475

CONCLUSION

With our recipe book "**Keto Ice Cream**", you can cook delicious and healthy low-carb frozen sweets for your family every day.

Many simple recipes for low-carb keto fruity, chocolate and other ice cream from the available products will diversify your daily diet.

No need to give up your favorite frozen sweets; just start cooking delicious homemade ice cream low in carbohydrates, which will help you to stay in good physical shape and to please itself and the guests with new recipes.

This collection of recipes will become a faithful assistant in your kitchen. Be inspired by the dishes presented and create your own culinary masterpieces!

Copyright © by Julia Patel

All rights reserved. No part of this publication may be reproduced, distributed, or transmitted in any form or by any means, including photocopying, recording, or other electronic or mechanical methods, without the prior written permission of the publisher, except in the case of brief quotations embodied in critical reviews and certain other noncommercial uses permitted by copyright law.

Disclaimer and Terms of Use: Effort has been made to ensure that the information in this book is accurate and complete, however, the author and the publisher do not warrant the accuracy of the information, text and graphics contained within the book due to the rapidly changing nature of science, research, known and unknown facts and internet. The Author and the publisher do not hold any responsibility for errors, omissions or contrary interpretation of the subject matter herein. This book is presented solely for motivational and informational purposes only.

Lightning Source UK Ltd.
Milton Keynes UK
UKHW052158110522
402781UK00015B/2058